M000223304

فوائد الذكر وثمراته

THE BENEFITS AND FRUITS OF

D H I K R

The Legislated Remembrances of Allāh

Shaykh `Abdur-Razzāq Ibn `Abdul-Muḥsin al-`Abbād al-Badr

© Maktabatulirshad Publications, USA

All rights reserved. No part of this publication may be reproduced in any language, stored in any retrieval system or transmitted in any form or by any means, whether electronic, mechanic, photocopying, recording or otherwise, without the express permission of the copyright owner.

ISBN: 978-1-6425-5862-3

First Edition: Rabī' Thāni 1439 A.H. /January 2018 C.E.

Cover Design: Usul Designs

Translation by 'Abdullāh Bin 'Ali Somali
Revision & Editing by 'Abdullāh Omrān

Typesetting & formatting by
Abū Sulaymān Muḥammad 'Abdul-'Aẓīm Ibn Joshua Baker

Subject: Fiqh/Admonition

Website: www.maktabatulirshad.com
E-mail: info@maktabatulirshad.com

مكتبة الإرشاد
Maktabatul-Irshad
PUBLICATIONS

CONTENTS

BRIEF BIOGRAPHY OF THE AUTHOR

His name: Shaykh 'Abdur-Razzāq Ibn 'Abdul-Muḥsin al-'Abbād al-Badr.

He is the son of the *'Allāmah* and *Muhaddith* of Madīnah Shaykh 'Abdul-Muḥsin al 'Abbād al-Badr.

Birth: He was born on the 22nd day of *Dhul-Qa'dah* in the year 1382 AH in az-Zal'fi, Kingdom of Saudi Arabia. He currently resides in Madīnah.

Current Occupation: He is a member of the teaching staff at the Islāmic University of Madīnah.

Scholarly Certifications: Doctorate in *'Aqīdah*.

The Shaykh has authored books, papers of research, as well as numerous explanations in different disciplines. Among them are:

1. *Fiqh of Supplications & adh-Adhkār.*

2. *Ḥajj & Refinement of Souls.*

3. Explanation of 'Exemplary Principles' by Shaykh Ibn 'Uthaymīn (رَحِمَهُ ٱللَّهُ).

4. Explanation of the book, *The Principles of Names & Attributes*, authored by Shaykh-ul-Islām Ibn al-Qayyim (رَحِمَهُ ٱللَّهُ).

5. Explanation of the book, *Good Words*, authored by Shaykh-ul-Islām Ibn al-Qayyim (رَحِمَهُ ٱللَّهُ).

6. Explanation of the book, al- 'Aqīdah *at-Tahāwiyyah*.

7. Explanation of the book, *al-Fuṣūl: Biography of the Messenger*, by Ibn Kathīr (رَحِمَهُ ٱللَّهُ).

8. An explanation of the book, *al-Adab-ul-Mufrad*, authored by Imām Bukhārī (رَحِمَهُ ٱللَّهُ).

He studied knowledge under several scholars. The most distinguished of them are:

1. His father the 'Allāmah Shaykh 'Abdul-Muhsin al-Badr (حفظه الله).

2. The 'Allāmah Shaykh Ibn Bāz (رَحِمَهُ ٱللَّهُ).

3. The 'Allāmah Shaykh Muḥammad ibn Sālih al-'Uthaymīn (رَحِمَهُ ٱللَّهُ).

4. Shaykh ʿAlī Ibn Nāsir al-Faqīhi (حفظه الله).

TRANSLITERATION TABLE

Consonants

ء	ʾ	د	d	ض	ḍ	ك	k
ب	b	ذ	dh	ط	ṭ	ل	l
ت	t	ر	r	ظ	ẓ	م	m
ث	th	ز	z	ع	ʿ	ن	n
ج	j	س	s	غ	gh	هـ	h
ح	ḥ	ش	sh	ف	f	و	w
خ	kh	ص	ṣ	ق	q	ي	y

Vowels

Short	ـَ	a	ـِ	i	ـُ	u
Long	ـَا	ā	ـِي	ī	ـُو	ū
Diphthongs	ـَوْ	aw	ـَيْ	ay

Arabic Symbols & their meanings

حفظه الله

May Allāh preserve him

رَضِيَ ٱللَّهُ عَنْهُ

May Allāh be pleased with him (i.e. a male companion of the Prophet Muḥammad)

سُبْحَانَهُ وَتَعَالَى

Glorified & Exalted is Allāh

(عَزَّوَجَلَّ)

(Allāh) the Mighty & Sublime

تَبَارَكَ وَتَعَالَى

(Allāh) the Blessed & Exalted

جَلَّ وَعَلَا

(Allāh) the Sublime & Exalted

عَلَيْهِ ٱلصَّلَاةُ وَٱلسَّلَامُ

May Allāh send Blessings & Safety upon him (i.e. a Prophet or Messenger)

صَلَّى ٱللَّهُ عَلَيْهِ وَعَلَىٰ آلِهِ وَسَلَّمَ	May Allāh send Blessings & Safety upon him and his family (i.e. Duʿā sent when mentioning the Prophet Muḥammad)
رَحِمَهُ ٱللَّهُ	May Allāh have mercy on him
رَضِيَ ٱللَّهُ عَنْهُمْ	May Allāh be pleased with them (i.e. Duʿā made for the Companions of the Prophet Muḥammad)
جَلَّ جَلَالُهُ	(Allāh) His Majesty is Exalted
رَضِيَ ٱللَّهُ عَنْهَا	May Allāh be pleased with her (i.e. a female companion of the Prophet Muḥammad)

INTRODUCTION

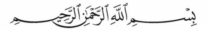

I praise and thank Allāh; the Most Generous, with his praiseworthy attributes that He is deserving of and I praise Him for all good. I cannot enumerate His praises; He is as He has praised Himself. All abundant, good, and blessed praise as much as the heavens, earth, and whatever after that is for Allāh, just as it is beloved and pleasing to our Lord. I praise Him for His many blessings, plentiful favors, and tremendous gifts. All praise and virtue belong to Him, and the entire affair returns to Him.

All the praises and thanks are to Allāh, to Whom belongs all that is in the heavens and all that is in the earth. His is all the praises and thanks in the Hereafter, and He is the All-Wise, the All-Aware:

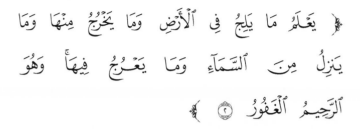

"He knows that which goes into the earth and
that which comes forth from it, and that which
descend from the heaven and that which
ascends to it. And He is the Most Merciful, the
Oft-Forgiving." [*Sūrah Saba* 34:2]

All the praises and thanks be to Allah, the Lord of the
'Ālamīn (mankind, jinn and all that exists). The Most
Gracious, the Most Merciful. The Only Owner (and the
Only Ruling Judge) of the Day of Recompense (i.e. the
Day of Resurrection). And I testify that there is no God
worthy of worship except Allah alone – He has no
partners – the God of the early and later generations,
the Self Subsisting One upon whom the heavens and
earths depend and the Maker of all of the creation. And
I testify that Muhammad is His servant, Messenger,
Sincere and close friend, trustee with His revelation
and conveyer of His legislation to the people. May the

INTRODUCTION

Salawāt and peace from Allāh be upon him and his entire family and companions.

THE IMPORTANCE OF *DHIKR* (REMEMBRANCE OF ALLĀH)

As for what follows:

Verily, the topic of the '*Dhikr*'[1](Remembrance) of Allāh – (عَزَّوَجَلَّ) – is tied to the most important, the greatest, most magnificent and foremost of affairs that we should give concern and care to; for it is concerning the *Dhikr* of Allāh The Magnificent, the remembrance of The Lord of the heavens and earth and all of creation, the remembrance of The Maker of the creation and The originator of all the people; the remembrance of Allāh, glorified is His affair, and

---

[1] **Translator's note:** Shaykh Muhammad al-'Uthaymīn – رَحِمَهُٱللَّه – said that *Dhikr* is every type of speech which will get you closer to Allāh – The Mighty and Majestic – like the recitation of the Qur'ān, enjoining good, forbidding evil and teaching others. He also said: As for it's specific meaning, *Dhikr* is saying Subhānallāh, Allāhu Akbar, Lā ilāha illallāh, Alhamdulillāh and what is similar to this. (Nūr 'Alā ad-Darb, tape 206)

magnificent is His sovereignty and blessed is His name; remembrance of:

﴿ ٱلْمَلِكُ ٱلْقُـدُّوسُ ٱلسَّـلَـٰمُ ٱلْمُؤْمِنُ ٱلْمُهَيْمِنُ ٱلْعَزِيزُ ٱلْجَبَّارُ ٱلْمُتَكَبِّرُ سُبْحَٰنَ ٱللَّهِ عَمَّا يُشْرِكُونَ ۩ هُوَ ٱللَّهُ ٱلْخَٰلِقُ ٱلْبَارِئُ ٱلْمُصَوِّرُ لَهُ ٱلْأَسْمَآءُ ٱلْحُسْنَىٰ يُسَبِّحُ لَهُۥ مَا فِى ٱلسَّمَٰوَٰتِ وَٱلْأَرْضِ وَهُوَ ٱلْعَزِيزُ ٱلْحَكِيمُ ۩ ﴾

"The King, The Holy, The One Free from all defects, The Giver of security, The Watcher over His creatures, The All-Mighty, The Compeller, The Supreme. Glory be to Allāh! (High is He) Above all that they associate as partners with Him. He is Allāh, The Creator, The Inventor of all things, The Bestower of forms. To Him belong the Best Names. All that is in the heavens and the earth glorify Him. And He is The All-Mighty, The All-Wise."
[*Sūrah al-Hashr* 58:23-24]

Indeed, the *Dhikr* of Allāh — (جَلَّوَعَلَا) — is the best matter with which one spend his time doing. With the *Dhikr*

of Allāh – (جَلَّوَعَلَا) – the hearts of the believers become
tranquil, their souls become calm, their certainty
magnifies, and their *Ēmān* (faith) increases. The *Dhikr*
of Allāh – (جَلَّوَعَلَا) – is the symbol of happiness and the
path to success in this world and the hereafter; rather
all good, happiness, delight, pleasure and tranquility
in this world and the next is dependent on the
performance of the *Dhikr* of Allāh – (جَلَّوَعَلَا) – rather all
of the legislation and acts of obedience in totality were
legislated to establish the *Dhikr* of Allāh. Hence what
Allāh – (عَزَّوَجَلَّ) – has legislated for his servants from
Salāh, fasting, *Hajj* and other than that from the acts of
obedience is solely for establishing the remembrance
of Allāh.

Thus, it has been affirmed in a *Hadīth* from the
Messenger of Allāh – (صَلَّ ٱللَّهُ عَلَيْهِ وَسَلَّمَ) – that a man asked
him:

أَيُّ الْجِهَادِ أَعْظَمُ أَجْراً؟ قَالَ : أَكْثَرُهُمْ لِلَّهِ تَبَارَكَ وَ تَعَالَى ذِكْرًا
، قَالَ : فَأَيُّ الصَّائِمِينَ أَعْظَمُ أَجْرًا ؟ قَالَ : أَكْثَرُهُمْ لِلَّهِ تَبَارَكَ
وَ تَعَالَى ذِكْرًا ، ثُمَّ ذَكَرَ لَنَا الصَّلَاةَ ، وَ الزَّكَاةَ ، وَ الْحَجَّ ، وَ
الصَّدَقَةَ كُلُّ ذَلِكَ رَسُولُ اللهِ صَلَّى اللهُ عَلَيْهِ وَ سَلَّم يَقُولُ :

THE IMPORTANCE OF DHIKR (REMEMBRANCE OF ALLĀH)

أَكْثَرُهُمْ لِلّٰهِ تَبَارَكَ وَ تَعَالَى ذِكْرًا . فَقَالَ أَبُو بَكْرٍ لِعُمَرَ : يَا أَبَا حَفْصٍ ذَهَبَ الذَّاكِرُونَ بِكُلِّ خَيْرٍ ، فَقَالَ رَسُولُ اللّٰهِ صَلَّى اللّٰهُ عَلَيْهِ وَ سَلَّمَ : أَجَلْ .

"Which Jihād is greater in reward?" He replied: "The one in which they make the most *Dhikr* of Allāh – (تَبَارَكَوَتَعَالَى). He [then] asked: "Who from amongst those fasting are greater in reward?" He said: "The ones who make *Dhikr* of Allāh – (تَبَارَكَوَتَعَالَى) – the most." Then he mentioned to us the *Salāh*, *Zakāh*, *Hajj* and *Sadaqah* (charity) and the Messenger of Allāh – (صَلَّىاللَّهُعَلَيْهِوَسَلَّمَ) – would say regarding all of them: "The ones that are most in making *Dhikr* of Allāh – (تَبَارَكَوَتَعَالَى)." So Abū Bakr said to 'Umar: "O Abū Hafs the *Dhākirūn* (the ones that make *Dhikr*) have taken all the good." The Messenger of Allāh – (صَلَّىاللَّهُعَلَيْهِوَسَلَّمَ) – replied: "Certainly!"[2]

---

[2] Reported by Ahmad (15614) and at-Tabarānī in *ad-Du'ā* (1887) and it includes (i.e., it's chain of narration) Zabān Ibn Fā'id and he is weak, but however, it has an authentic *Mursal* evidence reported by Ibn al-Mubārak in *az-Zuhd* (1429)

So, the *Dhākirūn* are the ones deserving most of earning
the magnificent rewards, elevated levels and lofty
stations in paradise. The *Dhikr* of Allāh is the soul and
the life of the hearts and the cause of its development
and strength; and abundant rewards and immense
good in this world and the next — whose count cannot
be enumerated except by Allāh — (جَلَّ وَعَلَا) — are a direct
result of it (i.e. *Dhikr*). For this reason, the topic of the
remembrance of Allāh — (سُبْحَانَهُ وَتَعَالَى) — is from the most
significant of topics and the one deserving most of
being given concern and importance.

KEEP YOUR TONGUE MOIST WITH THE *DHIKR* OF ALLĀH

In a *Hadīth*, the Prophet (ﷺ) said:

لَا يَزَالُ لِسَانُكَ رَطْبًا مِنْ ذِكْرِ اللهِ

"Keep your tongue wet with the remembrance of Allāh." It was reported by Imām Ahmad and other than him, and it is an authentic firm *Hadīth*.[3]

The story of the *Hadīth*): A man—as reported by ʿAbdullāh Ibn Busr— (رَضِيَٱللَّهُعَنهُ)—the narrator of the *Hadīth*—came to the Prophet— (عَلَيهِٱلصَّلَاةُوَٱلسَّلَامُ)—and said to him:

---

[3] *Al-Musnad* (17698) and it's been reported by at-Tirmidhī (3375), Ibn Mājah (3793) and al-Hākim (1/672) and he authenticated it from the *Hadīth* of ʿAbdullāh ibn Busr— (رَضِيَٱللَّهُعَنهُ)—and al-Albāni said it is authentic in *Sahīh al-Jāmiʿ* (7700):

إِنَّ شَرَائِعَ الإِسْلاَم قَدْ كَثُرَتْ عَلَيَّ فَأَخْبِرْنِي بِشَيْءٍ أَتَشَبَّثُ بِهِ

"O Messenger of Allāh, the injunctions of
Islām have become many for me. So tell me
something to which I may hold fast."

In another wording:

إِنَّ شَرَائِعَ الْإِسْلاَم قَدْ كَثُرَتْ عَلَيْنَا، فَبَابٌ نَتَمَسَّكُ بِهِ جَامِعٌ؟

"...the injunctions of Islām have become
many for us, so is there one encompassing
type?"

Like this, he asked the Prophet – (عَلَيْهِٱلصَّلَاةُوَٱلسَّلَامُ) – saying:

شَرَائِعَ الْإِسْلاَم قَدْ كَثُرَتْ

"The legislation of Islām have become too many,"
meaning, they've become too numerous for me, so I
want one that encompasses everything that is good so
that I can adhere to. He – (عَلَيْهِٱلصَّلَاةُوَٱلسَّلَامُ) – replied:

لَا يَزَالُ لِسَانُكَ رَطْبًا مِنْ ذِكْرِ اللهِ

KEEP YOUR TONGUE MOIST WITH THE DHIKR OF ALLĀH

"Let your tongue remain wet with the *Dhikr* of Allāh." The questioner wanted an all-inclusive aspect from the good that he could hold fast to. Hence the trustworthy and sincere advisor — (عَلَيْهِ ٱلصَّلَاةُ وَٱلسَّلَامُ) — directed him to the remembrance of Allāh — (جَلَّ وَعَلَا).

DHIKR IS FROM THE EASIEST AND SIMPLEST OF DEEDS

So reflect here – O reader – the guidance of the Prophet – (عَلَيْهِٱلصَّلَاةُوَٱلسَّلَامُ) – to the one whom the injunctions of Islām have become too numerous and varied and thus wanted an encompassing matter to adhere to that would actualize for him his happiness and allow him to earn the good of this life and the hereafter; and so he – (صَلَّىٱللَّهُعَلَيْهِوَسَلَّمَ) – instructed him with the easiest of deeds to load up on and perform that would earn him tremendous rewards and much good he wouldn't be able to amass with other than it.

The people of knowledge say: "Indeed, *Dhikr* – even if it is numerous and varied – is the lightest and easiest of deeds and it does not require much effort from the one performing it because the movement of the tongue with the remembrance of ar-Rahmān – (جَلَّوَعَلَا) – is not difficult and overtaxing on the tongue nor does it tire or toil one; rather, it causes tranquility, pleasure, and calmness of the heart and brings about the means of happiness.

DHIKR IS FROM THE EASIEST AND SIMPLEST OF DEEDS

When the deeds of the tongue are compared to those of the limbs such as *Salāh*, walking to the *Masājid*, ablution, *Hajj*, fasting and other than these, you'll find that they may contain some form of difficulty — a difficulty that might be dependent on the person. As for the remembrance of Allāh — (جَلَّوَعَلَا) — than it does not require anything from anybody, whether young or old, healthy or sick, male or female. A person is able to move his tongue with this good (i.e., *Dhikr*) in making *Tasbeeh* of Allāh (saying SubhānAllāh), thanking Allāh, remembering Allāh and praising Him while not tiring himself and actually earning a great deal of rewards and good in this life and the next that only Allāh — Subhānu Wa (سُبْحَانَهُوَتَعَالَى) — knows the worth of.

Thus, he — (عَلَيْهِٱلصَّلَاةُوَٱلسَّلَامُ) — said as in the *Sahīhayn* (*al-Bhukārī* and *Muslim*)[4]:

$$كَلِمَتَانِ خَفِيفَتَانِ عَلَى اللِّسَانِ$$

"Two words that are light on the tongue..." Notice that as soon as he started, he said:

---

[4] *al-Bukhāri* (6406, 6682 and 7563) and Muslim (2694) from the *Hadīth* of Abū Hurairah — (رَضِيَٱللَّهُعَنْهُ).

كَلِمَتَانِ خَفِيفَتَانِ عَلَى اللِّسَانِ

"Two words that are light on the tongue,"
highlighting their lightness, ease, and simplicity and
that they do not exhaust the one uttering them. But
what did he say after that? [He said]:

ثَقِيلَتَانِ فِي الْـمِيزَانِ ، حَبِيبَتَانِ إِلَى الرَّحْمَنِ

"heavy on the scale, beloved to ar-Rahmān." Their
weight is tremendous with Allāh; they are simple and
beautiful words and sweet on the tongue but heavy on
the scale and beloved to ar-Rahmān — (سُبْحَانَهُ وَتَعَالَى).

He also said:

مَنْ قَالَ: سُبْحَانَ اللهِ وَ بِحَمْدِهِ مِائَةَ مَرَّةٍ ؛ غُفِرَتْ لَهُ ذُنُوبُهُ ، وَ
إِنْ كَانَتْ مِثْلَ زَبَدِ الْـبَحْرِ

"Whoever says: *SubhānaAllāhi Wa bi Hamdihī*
(How perfect Allāh is, and I praise him) a

hundred times, his sins will be forgiven even if they were as much the foam of the sea."[5]

The *Dhikr* of Allāh is light on the tongue for whoever Allāh — (تَبَارَكَوَتَعَالَ) — aids and provides him with His *Tawfeeq*.

As for the one whom Allāh abandons — and refuge is sought with Allāh — then the *Dhikr* of Allāh will be difficult for him and he will not be able to make the *Dhikr* of Allāh, rather he will find it hard or possibly become annoyed and bored with *Dhikr*; and this is among the signs of being forsaken and a proof of deprivation — and refuge is with Allāh.

So, the *Dhikr* of Allāh is indeed light on the tongue and consequently the Prophet — (عَلَيْهِٱلصَّلَاةُوَٱلسَّلَامُ) — directed this questioner saying:

لَا يَزَالُ لِسَانُكَ رَطْبًا مِنْ ذِكْرِ اللهِ جَلَّ وَ عَلَا

"Let your tongue remain wet with the remembrance of Allāh — (جَلَّوَعَلَا)."

---

[5] Reported by Ahmad (8873), at-Tirmidhī (3466) and Ibn Mājah (3812) from the *Hadīth* of Abū Hurairah — (رَضِيَٱللَّهُعَنْهُ) — and at-Tirmidhī said it is: *Hasan Sahīh*.

He urged him — (عَلَيْهِٱلصَّلَاةُوَٱلسَّلَامُ) — to give concern to *Dhikr*
and in this is proof for the greatness of the matter of
Dhikr and the greatness of its status with Allāh —
(جَلَّوَعَلَا) — and that it is an all-inclusive door of goodness
that every *Muslim* should strictly hold fast to and be
from its people.

And if we combine this great *Hadīth* with the other
Ahādīth (plural of *Hadīth*) of the Prophet —
(عَلَيْهِٱلصَّلَاةُوَٱلسَّلَامُ) — and the texts from the Noble *Qur'ān* that
encourage with the performance of *Dhikr*, clarify its
virtues, greatness of its reward and what Allāh —
(تَبَارَكَوَتَعَالَ) — has prepared for the Dhākirūn, as well as
what results from making *Dhikr* from the tremendous
benefits, noble fruits and numerous good in this world
and the next, we will find in these texts many proofs
that show the enormity of the affair of this act of
obedience, the magnificence of its worth and the
loftiness of its status with Allāh — (تَبَارَكَوَتَعَالَ).

AN ENDORSEMENT FOR A GREAT BOOK

Imām Ibn al-Qayyim al-Jawziyyah — (رَحِمَهُٱللَّهُ) — has an unparalleled book on this topic. No one has written — to my knowledge — anything like it. It is a truly splendid treatise that is widely available amongst the people of knowledge and the students of knowledge which he — (رَحِمَهُٱللَّهُ) — titled: *al-Wābil as-Sayyib Fī al-Kalim at-Tayyib* and *al-Wābil as-Sayyib* means *The Beneficial Rain*. He said in this treatise: "Contained in *Dhikr* is more than a hundred benefits," he — (رَحِمَهُٱللَّهُ) — then started counting the benefits of *Dhikr* and its fruits in this world and the hereafter. He mentioned more than seventy benefits of *Dhikr*, each point sufficing in moving the hearts and exciting the souls to perform this great act of obedience — so imagine if all of them were to come together. Thus, it is rare to find a Muslim who reads this book — doing a close reading and hoping to benefit — except that his state with the *Dhikr* of Allāh — (جَلَّوَعَلَا) — will become better — by the will of Allāh — and his concern for this topic will increase.

So, when he finished listing the benefits of *Dhikr* and explained them in length, he moved on to mention chapters on the types of *Dhikr* that a *Muslim* should observe.

Just when the *Muslim* finishes with this 'powerful push' – if such a term is correct – to perform the *Dhikr* of Allāh, he finds in front of him another detailed section on the types of *Dhikr* taken from the Book of Allāh and the *Sunnah* of Prophet – (صَلَّى ٱللَّهُ عَلَيْهِ وَعَلَىٰٓ آلِهِ وَسَلَّمَ).

Hence, in my opinion, it is befitting for every *Muslim* to give concern to this book. The father should concern himself with buying it and giving it as a gift to his children and wife at home, and he should encourage them to read it. The student should likewise be diligent in getting it and benefiting from it. Also, it should be circulated amongst the Muslims due to the greatness and magnitude of its benefits.

And from this treatise, I will summarize some of the benefits of *Dhikr* from what he – (رَحِمَهُٱللَّهُ) – lists along with the benefits above at the beginning of the talk.

THE BENEFITS OF *DHIKR*:

DHIKR IS IN FACT LIFE FOR THE HEARTS

From the benefits of *Dhikr* is that it is the true liveliness of the hearts and they will die without it. Thus it has been affirmed in the *Sahīh*[6] from the Prophet — (ﷺ) — that he said:

مَثَلُ الَّذِي يَذْكُرُ رَبَّهُ وَالَّذِي لاَ يَذْكُرُ مَثَلُ الْحَيِّ وَالْمَيِّتِ

"The similitude of the one who remembers his Lord and the one who does not remember his Lord is like that of the living and the dead,"

and in another wording of the *Hadīth*, he said:

---

[6] Reported by al-Bukhāri (6407) from the *Hadīth* of Abū Mūsā al-Ash'ari — (ﷺ).

مَثَلُ الْبَيْتِ الَّذِي يُذْكَرُ اللَّهُ فِيهِ وَالْبَيْتِ الَّذِي لاَ يُذْكَرُ اللَّهُ

فِيهِ مَثَلُ الْحَيِّ وَالْمَيِّتِ

"The similitude of the house in which the
remembrance of Allāh is made and the one in
which Allāh is not remembered is like that of
the living and the dead."[7]

So he — (عَلَيْهِٱلصَّلَاةُوَٱلسَّلَامُ) — made the one who remembers
Allāh like the living and the houses of those who
remember Allāh like the houses of the living and he —
(عَلَيْهِٱلصَّلَاةُوَٱلسَّلَامُ) — made the one who doesn't make *Dhikr*
of Allāh like the dead and the houses of those who
don't remember Allāh like the houses of the dead and
they are the graveyards.

Consequently, he said in another *Hadīth*:

لَا تَجْعَلُوا بُيُوتَكُمْ مَقَابِرَ

"Do not make your homes graveyards,"[8]

---

[7] Reported by *Muslim* (7789)
[8] Reported by Muslim (780) from the *Hadīth* of Abū Hurairah —
(رَضِيَٱللَّهُعَنْهُ).

meaning make *Dhikr* and remember your lord in your homes, establish the prayer and recite the words of Allāh (i.e., the *Qur'ān*); because if the words of Allāh are not recited in a home, Allāh is not remembered and the *Salāh* is not established, it will be like the homes of the dead which are the cemeteries.

Accordingly, he — (عَلَيْهِ ٱلصَّلَاةُوَٱلسَّلَامُ) — encouraged us with the optional prayers in the houses saying:

إِنَّ أَفْضَلَ الصَّلَاةِ صَلَاةُ الْـمَرْءِ فِي بَيْتِهِ إِلَّا الْـمَكْتُوبَةَ

"Verily, the best *Salāh* (prayer) of a man is the *Salāh* performed in his home except for the obligatory prayers,"[9]

This is so that the home does not become a graveyard. The home in which Allāh — (جَلَّوَعَلَا) — is not mentioned, nor is the *Salāh* performed, nor is Allāh — (سُبْحَانَهُوَتَعَالَى) — is praised and thanked, is like the cemetery, the home of the dead.

---

[9] Reported by al-Bukhārī (731) from the *Hadīth* of Zaid Ibn Thābit — (رَضِيَٱللَّهُعَنْهُ).

And how is the case in the house in which only the devils are remembered, only amusement and musical instruments are listened to and Allāh – (جَلَّ وَعَلَا) – is not remembered?! Rather it is populated with tools of entertainment and wickedness and sounds of falsehood and what is similar to that – this is a dead house – it is utter destruction! And the ruined houses are only inhabited and visited by the devils – and refuge is sought with Allāh. As for the angles, they will not enter such homes, rather the devils will enter into them successively, and it will be a haven for them. As a result, the good will depart from such a home, the evil will increase, problems will arise in succession, calamities will increase, and all the different types of immorality will occur in it – and refuge is sought with Allāh. Allāh – (جَلَّ وَعَلَا) – says:

﴿ وَمَن يَعْشُ عَن ذِكْرِ ٱلرَّحْمَٰنِ نُقَيِّضْ لَهُۥ شَيْطَٰنًا فَهُوَ لَهُۥ قَرِينٌ ۝٣٦ وَإِنَّهُمْ لَيَصُدُّونَهُمْ عَنِ ٱلسَّبِيلِ وَيَحْسَبُونَ أَنَّهُم مُّهْتَدُونَ ۝٣٧ ﴾

"And whosoever turns away blindly from the remembrance of the Most Gracious (Allāh) (i.e. this Qur'ān and worship of Allāh), We appoint for him Shayṭān (Satan) to be a Qarīn (an intimate companion) to him. And verily, they (devils) hinder them from the Path (of Allāh), but they think that they are guided aright!" [*Sūrah az-Zukhruf* 43:36-37]

So it is mandatory upon the people of the believing homes that they be sincere towards and advise themselves and their homes; and thus populate it with the *Dhikr* of Allāh — (جَلَّوَعَلَا) — with the recitation of the Qur'ān, the establishment of the *Salāh* and the performance of the good deeds so that their home will be from the homes of the living and they themselves will be alive in a vibrant home. So the *Dhikr* of Allāh — (جَلَّوَعَلَا) — is the true liveliness of the hearts, and without it, the hearts will perish.

Ibn al-Qayyim — (رَحِمَهُ ٱللَّه) — reported from his Shaykh, the Shaykh of Islām, Ibn Taymiyyah — (رَحِمَهُ ٱللَّه) — an amazing similitude for *Dhikr* and the state of the heart with *Dhikr*. Ibn Taymiyyah said:

"*Dhikr* for the heart is like water for fish. What
will be the state of a fish if it is separated from
water?"[10]

And it is well-known that if a fish is taken out of water
for a few moments, it will die; and if the heart is
distanced from *Dhikr* and it is occupied with the *Dhikr*
of Allāh – (تَبَارَكَوَتَعَالَ) – it will die. Life will not develop in
it except with the *Dhikr* of Allāh. Hence, Allāh –
(سُبْحَانَهُوَتَعَالَ) – said:

$$ \text{يَٰٓأَيُّهَا ٱلَّذِينَ ءَامَنُوٓاْ ٱسۡتَجِيبُواْ لِلَّهِ وَلِلرَّسُولِ} $$
$$ \text{إِذَا دَعَاكُمۡ لِمَا يُحۡيِيكُمۡ} $$

"O you who believe! Answer Allāh (by
obeying Him) and (His) Messenger when he
((صَلَّاللَّهُعَلَيْهِوَسَلَّمَ)) calls you to that which will give
you life." [*Sūrah al-'Anfāl* 8:24]

Allāh – (تَبَارَكَوَتَعَالَ) – has called the Revelation '*Rūh*' (a
soul) in many places in the Qur'ān as in His statement:

---

[10] *al-Waabil as-Sayyib* (85)

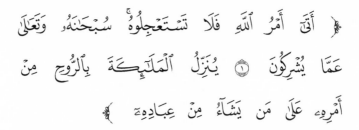

﴿ أَتَىٰٓ أَمْرُ ٱللَّهِ فَلَا تَسْتَعْجِلُوهُ سُبْحَنَهُۥ وَتَعَلَىٰ عَمَّا يُشْرِكُونَ ۝ يُنَزِّلُ ٱلْمَلَٰٓئِكَةَ بِٱلرُّوحِ مِنْ أَمْرِهِۦ عَلَىٰ مَن يَشَآءُ مِنْ عِبَادِهِۦٓ ﴾

"The Event (the Hour or the punishment of disbelievers and polytheists or the Islāmic laws or commandments), ordained by Allāh will come to pass, so seek not to hasten it. Glorified and Exalted be He above all that they associate as partners with Him. He sends down the angels with Rūh (revelation) of His Command to whom of His slaves He wills." [*Sūrah an-Nahl* 16:1-2]

Also, in His statement:

﴿ وَكَذَٰلِكَ أَوْحَيْنَآ إِلَيْكَ رُوحًا مِّنْ أَمْرِنَا مَا كُنتَ تَدْرِى مَا ٱلْكِتَٰبُ وَلَا ٱلْإِيمَٰنُ وَلَٰكِن جَعَلْنَٰهُ نُورًا نَّهْدِى بِهِۦ مَن نَّشَآءُ مِنْ عِبَادِنَا ﴾

"And thus We have sent to you (O Muḥammad
(ﷺ)) Rūh (a Revelation, and a Mercy) of
Our Command. You knew not what is the
Book, nor what is Faith. But We have made it
(this Qur'ān) a light wherewith We guide
whosoever of Our slaves We will." [Sūrah ash-
Shūrā 42:52]

Allāh — (تَبَارَكَوَتَعَالَى) — has (similarly) called the one who
descends with the Revelations — who is Jibrīl — a 'Rūh.'
He said:

"Which the trustworthy Rūh [Jibrīl (Gabriel)]
has brought down; Upon your heart (O
Muhammad (ﷺ)) that you may be (one)
of the warners, In the plain Arabic language."
[Sūrah ash-Shu'arā 26:193-195]

So, Jibrīl — (عَلَيْهِٱلسَّلَامُ) — the one who descends with the
Revelation — is a 'Rūh' and the Revelation itself is a
'Rūh,' because the heart will not be alive without the
Revelation and the Dhikr of Allāh — (تَبَارَكَوَتَعَالَى) — and

without it: it will die, become hard and oppressive and it will be populated by evil and corruption — and refuge is sought with Allāh. However, if the Revelation reaches it and it becomes occupied with the *Dhikr* of Allāh — (جَلَّوَعَلَا) — goodness and righteousness develop and increase in it, and it will be enveloped by benefits and blessings — this is a tremendous benefit from the benefits of *Dhikr*.

DHIKR REPELS THE DEVIL

From the benefits of *Dhikr* is that it expels the devil, pushes him away from the person and the believer — with the *Dhikr* of Allāh — (تَبَارَكَوَتَعَالَى) — will be in an impenetrable fortress and a strong shelter that the devil cannot find an entrance to.

There is a *Hadīth* reported by Imām 'Aḥmad in *al-Musnad* and other than him with an authentic chain of narration that the Prophet — (صَلَّ ٱللَّهُ عَلَيْهِ وَسَلَّمَ) — said:

إِنَّ اللهَ عَزَّ وَ جَلَّ أَمَرَ يَحْيى بنَ زَكَرِيَا عَلَيْهِمَا السَّلَامُ بِخَمْسِ كَلِمَاتٍ أَنْ يَعْمَلَ بِهِنَّ، وَ أَنْ يَأْمُرَ بَنِي إِسْرَائِيلَ أَنْ يَعْمَلُوا بِهِنَّ

"Verily, Allāh — (عَزَّوَجَلَّ) — commanded Yahyā Ibn Zakariyyā — (عَلَيْهِمَاٱلسَّلَامْ) — with five commandments to abide by, and to command the Children of Isra'il to abide by them."

And in the *Hadīth*, Zakariyyā said to his people:

إِنَّ رَبِّي أَمَرَنِي بِخَمْسِ كَلِمَاتٍ وَ أَمَرَنِي أَنْ آمُرَكُمْ بِهِنَّ

"Verily, my Lord instructed me with five commandments, and He ordered me to instruct you with it,"

Then he mentioned the command firstly with *Tawhīd* (singling Allāh alone in worship), *Salāh*, charity, then he mentioned the fifth command: command with the *Dhikr* of Allāh, so he said:

وَ آمُرُكُمْ بِذِكْرِ اللهِ عَزَّ وَ جَلَّ كَثِيرًا، وَ إِنَّ مَثَلَ ذَلِكَ كَمَثَلِ رَجُلٍ طَلَبَهُ الْعَدُوُّ سِرَاعًا فِي أَثَرِهِ

"I command you to make the remembrance of Allāh — (عَزَّوَجَلَّ) — in abundance; and verily, the similitude of this is like a man who is quickly tracked by the enemy,"

Meaning, the enemy caught up to him to kill and destroy him,

فَأَتَى حِصْنًا حَصِينًا ، فَتَحَصَّنَ فِيهِ ، وَ إِنَّ الْعَبْدَ أَحْصَنُ مَا

يَكُونُ مِنَ الشَّيْطَانِ إِذَا كَانَ فِي ذِكْرِ اللهِ عَزَّ وَ جَلَّ

"so he comes to an impenetrable fortress and seeks protection from it. And the most fortified a servant can be from the devil is if he is occupied with the *Dhikr* of Allāh — (عَزَّوَجَلَّ)."[11]

So, the one who makes *Dhikr* of Allāh is in an unconquerable fortress and a strong shelter that the devil cannot break through or ever reach. Allāh — (سُبْحَانَهُوَتَعَالَى) — said:

﴿ قُلْ أَعُوذُ بِرَبِّ ٱلنَّاسِ ۝ مَلِكِ ٱلنَّاسِ ۝ إِلَٰهِ ٱلنَّاسِ ۝ مِن شَرِّ ٱلْوَسْوَاسِ ٱلْخَنَّاسِ ۝ ٱلَّذِى يُوَسْوِسُ فِى صُدُورِ ٱلنَّاسِ ۝ مِنَ ٱلْجِنَّةِ وَٱلنَّاسِ ۝ ﴾

---

[11] *al-Musnad* (17170) and it is also reported by at-Tirmidhī (2763) and al-Hākim (1/204, 582) from the *Hadīth* of al-Hārith al-Ash'arī — (رَضِيَاللهُعَنْهُ) — and it has been authenticated by al-Albānī in *Sahīh al-Jāmi'* (1724)

"Say: "I seek refuge with (Allāh) the Lord of mankind, "The King of mankind — "The Ilāh (God) of mankind, "From the evil of the whisperer (devil who whispers evil in the hearts of men) who withdraws (from his whispering in one's heart after one remembers Allāh) "Who whispers in the breasts of mankind, "Of jinn and men." [*Sūrah an-Nās 114:1-6*]

'al-Waswās al-Khannās' (The whisperer who withdraws): This is the attribute of the devil. Ibn 'Abbās — (رَضِىَاللَّهُعَنْهُ) — said regarding the meaning of these two words (The whisperer who withdraws):

"The devil crouches down on the heart of the son of Adam, so when he forgets and becomes heedless, he whispers to him; and if he remembers Allāh (makes *Dhikr*), he withdraws."[12]

When the servant makes *Dhikr* of his Lord, Satan withdraws, cringes and becomes like a fly; and he will

---

[12] Reported by at-Tabarī in his *Tafseer* (24/754), the Dār Hijr edition

not remain with the one making *Dhikr*, rather he flees from him. Thus, it has come in a *Hadīth*:

إِذَا نُودِيَ لِلصَّلَاةِ أَدْبَرَ الشَّيْطَانُ وَلَهُ ضُرَاطٌ

"When the call for *Salāh* is made, Satan retreats while passing wind."[13]

He cannot bear to hear the *Dhikr* of Allāh – (جَلَّوَعَلَا). The *Dhikr* actually harms and expels him, and he completely distances himself from a place in which the *Dhikr* of Allāh – (جَلَّوَعَلَا) – is made.

So, the one who makes *Dhikr* is in a well-fortified fortress and a strong, safe haven that will protect him by the will of Allāh – (تَبَارَكَوَتَعَالَى) – from the accursed devil. However, if he (the servant) is heedless, the devils will come to him in succession, push him to falsehood and strongly urge him to fall into sinning as has proceeded with us:

---

[13] Reported by al-Bukhārī (608) and Muslim (389) on the authority of Abū Hurairah – (رَضِيَاللَّهُعَنْهُ).

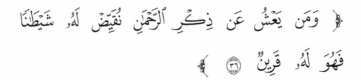

"And whosoever turns away blindly from the remembrance of the Most Gracious (Allāh) (i.e. this *Qur'ān* and worship of Allāh), We appoint for him Shaitān (Satan) to be a Qarīn (an intimate companion) to him." [*Sūrah az-Zukhruf* 43:36]

['Qarīn' (an intimate companion)] means that he is inseparable from him and does not leave him. The opposite understanding that can be taken from the *Āyah* is that: If (the servant) makes *Dhikr* of Allāh — (جَلَّوَعَلَا) — Satan will stay away from him; so *Dhikr* is a fortress from the accursed devil. Thus, whoever named his book on *Dhikr* from the people of knowledge *al-Hisn al-Haseen* (*The Impenetrable Fortress*) or *Hisnul Muslim* (The Fortress of the *Muslim*) or something similar to this, has done an excellent job. This is a true name (true to its meaning regarding what it contains) because *Dhikr* is an impenetrable fortress, it is the fortress of the *Muslim*, and it is the shelter in which a *Muslim* is protected — by the will of Allāh — (تَبَارَكَوَتَعَالَى).

And the devil will not find a path to the one who
makes *Dhikr* of Allāh – (جَلَّوَعَلَا) – at all times and in
everything. If you make *Dhikr* of Allāh when you are
about to eat, the devil will keep away from you, if you
make *Dhikr* of Allāh when you enter the home, the
devil will keep away from you, and like this for every
matter in which you make the *Dhikr* of Allāh –
(جَلَّوَعَلَا) – the devil will not have a way to get to you,
and you will be protected from his whispers, plots,
evil, prodding, and satanic poetry. This is a truly
magnificent benefit from the benefits of *Dhikr*.

DHIKR IS A SOURCE OF SERENITY FOR THE HEARTS

Also, from the benefits of *Dhikr* is that—as Allāh has mentioned—it is a cause for the tranquility of the heart. Allāh—(جَلَّوَعَلَا)—says:

﴿ أَلَا بِذِكْرِ ٱللَّهِ تَطْمَئِنُّ ٱلْقُلُوبُ ۝ ﴾

"Verily, in the remembrance of Allāh do hearts find rest." [*Sūrah ar-Rad* 13:28]

The tranquility of the heart is its pleasure, serenity, pleasantness and the absence of its worry, tension, annoyance and all the types of harm that might affect it. So those that make *Dhikr* of Allāh—(جَلَّوَعَلَا)—a lot, they are the people with tranquil hearts, happy hearts; the people whose hearts are filled with pleasantness and pleasure at all times—not just in the times of ease and happiness—rather in all situations. You will find him with a peaceful heart in times of ease and difficulty, in times of prosperity and poverty, in times of health and sickness. He will not be affected by worry, nor will he be stricken with anxiety and nor will he complain or be annoyed; rather you will find him calm, tranquil and comfortable at all times.

This is why, he — (عَلَيْهِ ٱلصَّلَاةُ وَٱلسَّلَامُ) — said in amazement:

عَجَبًا لأَمْرِ الْمُؤْمِنِ إِنَّ أَمْرَهُ كُلَّهُ خَيْرٌ وَلَيْسَ ذَاكَ لأَحَدٍ إِلاَّ لِلْمُؤْمِنِ إِنْ أَصَابَتْهُ سَرَّاءُ شَكَرَ فَكَانَ خَيْرًا لَهُ وَإِنْ أَصَابَتْهُ ضَرَّاءُ صَبَرَ فَكَانَ خَيْرًا لَهُ

"How wonderful is the case of the believer; there is good for him in everything, and this applies only to a believer: If he is granted prosperity, he is grateful — and this is better for him; and if he is afflicted with hardship, he endures it with patience, and this is better for him."[14] He — (عَلَيْهِ ٱلصَّلَاةُ وَٱلسَّلَامُ) — said it like this."

So the believer, he is in continuous harmony, with a calm heart and a cheerful breast and is full of joy. And all of this is a result of his adherence to the

---

[14] Reported by Muslim (2999) from the *Hadīth* of Suhayb — (رَضِيَ ٱللَّهُ عَنْهُ).

remembrance of Allāh — (جَلَّ وَعَلَا) — and his continuous
upon it, thus obtaining this serenity:

﴾ ٱلَّذِينَ ءَامَنُواْ وَتَطْمَئِنُّ قُلُوبُهُم بِذِكْرِ ٱللَّهِ أَلَا بِذِكْرِ
ٱللَّهِ تَطْمَئِنُّ ٱلْقُلُوبُ ۝ ﴿

**"Those who believed (in the Oneness of Allāh
- Islāmic Monotheism), and whose hearts find
rest in the remembrance of Allāh, Verily, in
the remembrance of Allāh do hearts find rest."**
[*Sūrah ar-Ra'ad* 13:28]

Their hearts find rest with the remembrance of Allāh
and not with anything else. They make *Dhikr* of
Allāh — (جَلَّ وَعَلَا) — in all of their situations:

﴾ ٱلَّذِينَ يَذْكُرُونَ ٱللَّهَ قِيَٰمًا وَقُعُودًا وَعَلَىٰ
جُنُوبِهِمْ ﴿

**"Those who remember Allāh (always, and in
prayers) standing, sitting, and lying down on
their sides."** [*Sūrah 'Āli 'Imrān* 3:191]

Meaning at all times: as a resident or traveler, while sitting, standing or walking; in all their affairs, they make *Dhikr* of Allāh – (جَلَّوَعَلَا) – and with this *Dhikr*, their hearts find rest:

"**Verily, in the remembrance of Allāh do hearts find rest.**" [*Sūrah ar-Ra'ad* 13:28]

DHIKR REMOVES HARDNESS OF THE HEART

From the benefits of *Dhikr* is that it removes the hardness of the heart. The heart can become hard because of sins and negligence in obedience to Allāh — (جَلَّ وَعَلَا) — and other similar factors. There is nothing that removes the hardness of the hearts as *Dhikr* does; and there is nothing greater in hardening the hearts than being heedless from the remembrance of Allāh — (جَلَّ وَعَلَا). Allāh — (سُبْحَانَهُ وَتَعَالَى) — said:

﴿ ۞ أَلَمْ يَأْنِ لِلَّذِينَ ءَامَنُوٓاْ أَن تَخْشَعَ قُلُوبُهُمْ لِذِكْرِ ٱللَّهِ وَمَا نَزَلَ مِنَ ٱلْحَقِّ وَلَا يَكُونُواْ كَٱلَّذِينَ أُوتُواْ ٱلْكِتَٰبَ مِن قَبْلُ فَطَالَ عَلَيْهِمُ ٱلْأَمَدُ فَقَسَتْ قُلُوبُهُمْ وَكَثِيرٌ مِّنْهُمْ فَٰسِقُونَ ۝ ﴾

"Has not the time come for the hearts of those who believe (in the Oneness of Allāh - Islāmic

Monotheism) to be affected by Allāh's Reminder (this Qur'ān), and that which has been revealed of the truth, lest they become as those who received the Scripture [the Taurāt (Torah) and the Injīl (Gospel)] before (i.e. Jews and Christians), and the term was prolonged for them and so their hearts were hardened? And many of them were Fāsiqūn (the rebellious, the disobedient to Allāh)." [*Sūrah al-Ḥadīd* 57:16]

The reason for the hardening of the hearts — as is evident from the noble Āyāh — is the lengthiness of the time that one was distant from making *Dhikr* and fulfilling the commands of Allāh — (تَبَارَكَوَتَعَالَ). So if this keeping away [from *Dhikr*] occurs, the hearts will harden, and it (the hardening) will not go away except by returning to the *Dhikr* of Allāh and to Allāh — (تَبَارَكَوَتَعَالَ). This is why Allāh says in the following Ayāh:

> **"Know that Allāh gives life to the earth after
> its death! Indeed We have made clear the Ayāt
> (proofs, evidence, verses, lessons, signs,
> revelations) to you if you but understand."**
> [*Sūrah al-Ḥadīd* 57:17]

"Allāh gives life to the earth after its death!"
Meaning, just as He — (سُبْحَانَهُوَتَعَالَى) — gives life to the
earth after its death with water and rain; He —
(تَبَارَكَوَتَعَالَى) — gives life to the dead hearts with the
Revelation and the remembrance of Allāh — (جَلَّوَعَلَا).
When the servant remembers his Lord, his heart will
come to life, and its hardness will go away. It is
reported that a man came to Imām al-Hasan al-Basri —
(رَحِمَهُٱللَّهُ) — and said to him:

> "O Abū Sa'īd! I am complaining to you about
> the hardness of my heart." He replied: "Melt it
> with the remembrance of Allāh,"[15]

Meaning: dissolve this hardness which is in your
heart with the *Dhikr* of Allāh — (تَبَارَكَوَتَعَالَى) — because the
Dhikr of Allāh removes the hardness which might

---

[15] Look in: *al-Waabil as-Sayyib* (142)

cover the heart and then the heart will soften and become calm and tranquil as has proceeded.

YOU WILL BE REMEMBERED BY ALLĀH

Also, from the benefits of *Dhikr* is that it earns the servant a certain magnificent benefit and a lofty station: If he remembers and mentions Allāh, Allāh— (سُبْحَانَهُوَتَعَالَى)—will remember him; because rewards, good or bad, are dependent on the basis of deed. Allāh- (سُبْحَانَهُوَتَعَالَى)—says:

$$ ﴿ هَلْ جَزَآءُ ٱلْإِحْسَٰنِ إِلَّا ٱلْإِحْسَٰنُ ۞ ﴾ $$

"Is there any reward for good other than good?" [*Sūrah ar-Rahmān* 55:60]

So whoever remembers Allāh, Allāh will remember him and whoever forgets about Allāh, Allāh will forget about him:

$$ ﴿ نَسُوا۟ ٱللَّهَ فَنَسِيَهُمْ ﴾ $$

"They have forgotten Allāh, so He has forgotten them." [*Sūrah at-Tawbah* 9:67]

And,

﴿ جَزَآءً وِفَاقًا ۝ ﴾

"An exact recompense (according to their evil crimes)." [*Sūrah* an-Naba' 78:26]

And,

﴿ ثُمَّ كَانَ عَٰقِبَةَ ٱلَّذِينَ أَسَٰٓـُٔواْ ٱلسُّوٓأَىٰٓ ﴾

"Then evil was the end of those who did evil." [*Sūrah ar-Room* 30:10]

So, the recompense is based on the type of deed; whoever remembers Allāh, Allāh will remember him. Allāh – (سُبْحَانَهُوَتَعَالَى) – said:

﴿ فَٱذۡكُرُونِيٓ أَذۡكُرۡكُمۡ ﴾

"Therefore remember Me (by praying, glorifying). I will remember you." [*Sūrah al-Baqarah* 2:152]

And in a *Hadīth*, the Messenger of Allāh —
(ﷺ) — mentions that his Lord — (تَبَارَكَ وَتَعَالَ) — said:

فَإِنْ ذَكَرَنِي فِي نَفْسِهِ ذَكَرْتُهُ فِي نَفْسِي، وَإِنْ ذَكَرَنِي فِي مَلَأٍ
ذَكَرْتُهُ فِي مَلَأٍ خَيْرٍ مِنْهُمْ

"...If he remembers Me inwardly, I will remember him inwardly, and if he remembers Me in an assembly, I will remember him in a better assembly (i.e., in the assembly of angels)."[16]

And what reward is better and what status is more magnificent and loftier than being mentioned and remembered by Allāh — (تَبَارَكَ وَتَعَالَ) — in the assembly of angels. He — (سُبْحَانَهُ وَتَعَالَ) — remembers you, yet He is in no need of you, but you remember Him because you are in desperate need of him. He — (سُبْحَانَهُ وَتَعَالَ) — remembers you in the assembly of the angels while He does not benefit whatsoever from remembering you. You remembering Him — (سُبْحَانَهُ وَتَعَالَ) — does not

---

16 Reported by al-Bukhārī (7405) and Muslim (2675) from the *Hadīth* of Abū Hurairah — (رَضِيَ اللَّهُ عَنْهُ).

increase His kingdom, nor does your abandoning his
Dhikr decrease His kingdom.

Thus, He – (تَبَارَكَ وَتَعَالَى) – says in the *Hadīth Qudsī*:

لَوْ أَنَّ أَوَّلَكُمْ وَآخِرَكُمْ وَإِنْسَكُمْ وَجِنَّكُمْ كَانُوا عَلَى أَتْقَى
قَلْبِ رَجُلٍ وَاحِدٍ مِنْكُمْ مَا زَادَ ذَلِكَ فِي مُلْكِي شَيْئًا يَا عِبَادِي
لَوْ أَنَّ أَوَّلَكُمْ وَآخِرَكُمْ وَإِنْسَكُمْ وَجِنَّكُمْ كَانُوا عَلَى أَفْجَرِ
قَلْبِ رَجُلٍ وَاحِدٍ مَا نَقَصَ ذَلِكَ مِنْ مُلْكِي شَيْئًا

**"O My servants, even if the first amongst you
and the last amongst you and even the whole
of the human race of yours, and that of the
Jinns, become (equal in) God-conscious like
the heart of a single person amongst you,
nothing of that would add to My Power. O My
servants, even if the first amongst you and the
last amongst you and the whole human race of
yours and that of the Jinns too in unison
become the most wicked (all beating) like the**

**heart of a single person, it would cause no loss
to My Power."[17]**

So, the obedience of the obedient ones does not benefit
him, nor does the disobedience of the sinners harm
Him — (تَبَارَكَوَتَعَالَى); and the *Dhikr* of those that remember
Him does not increase his sovereignty, nor does the
heedlessness of the heedless decrease anything from
his sovereignty. However, out of His kindness and
grace — (تَبَارَكَوَتَعَالَى) — for his servants, He mentions the
one that remembers Him in the assembly of the
angels. Whoever remembers Allāh inwardly, Allāh
will remember him inwardly, and whoever
remembers Allāh in an assembly, Allāh will
remember him in an assembly better than it.

It has been reported in *Sahīh Muslim* (2701) on the
authority of Mu'āwiyah — (رَضِيَٱللَّهُعَنْهُ) — that the
Messenger of Allāh — (صَلَّىٱللَّهُعَلَيْهِوَسَلَّمَ) — came to a
gathering of his companions and said:

---

[17] Reported by *Muslim* (2577) from the *Hadīth* of Abū Hurairah —
(رَضِيَٱللَّهُعَنْهُ).

مَا أَجْلَسَكُمْ قَالُوا جَلَسْنَا نَذْكُرُ اللَّهَ . قَالَ آللَّهِ مَا أَجْلَسَكُمْ

إِلاَّ ذَاكَ قَالُوا وَاللَّهِ مَا أَجْلَسَنَا إِلاَّ ذَاكَ . قَالَ أَمَا إِنِّي لَمْ

أَسْتَحْلِفْكُمْ تُهْمَةً لَكُمْ وَ لَكِنَّهُ أَتَانِي جِبْرِيلُ فَأَخْبَرَنِي أَنَّ

اللَّهَ عَزَّ وَ جَلَّ يُبَاهِي بِكُمُ الْـمَلَائِكَةَ

"What makes you sit?" They said: "We are sitting here in order to remember Allah and to praise Him for He guided us to the path of Islām and He conferred favors upon us." Thereupon he said: "By Allāh, is this what made you sit?" They said: "By Allāh, we are not sitting here but for this very purpose," whereupon he (the Messenger) said: "I am not asking you to take an oath because of any allegation against you but for the fact that Jibrīl came to me and he informed me that Allāh — (عَزَّوَجَلَّ) — was talking to the angels about your magnificence."

Allāh would boast about those making *Dhikr* to the angels, saying: Look at my servants. They have gathered to remember me. They have gathered to thank me. They have gathered to praise me. He would boast about them to the angels.

Hence, it has also been reported in the other *Hadīth* in *Sahīh Muslim*[18] that he — (عَلَيْهِٱلصَّلَاةُوَٱلسَّلَامُ) — said:

مَا اجْتَمَعَ قَوْمٌ فِي بَيْتٍ مِنْ بُيُوتِ اللَّهِ تَعَالَى يَتْلُونَ كِتَابَ اللَّهِ وَيَتَدَارَسُونَهُ بَيْنَهُمْ إِلاَّ نَزَلَتْ عَلَيْهِمُ السَّكِينَةُ وَغَشِيَتْهُمُ الرَّحْمَةُ وَحَفَّتْهُمُ الْمَلاَئِكَةُ وَذَكَرَهُمُ اللَّهُ فِيمَنْ عِنْدَهُ

"Any group of people that assemble in one of the Houses of Allāh to recite the Book of Allāh, learning and teaching it, tranquility will descend upon them, mercy will engulf them, angels will surround them, and Allah will make mention of them to those (the angels) in His proximity."

This is a lofty station and an elevated and superior status obtained by the one that makes *Dhikr* of Allāh — (تَبَارَكَوَتَعَالَى) — and it is that Allāh — (تَبَارَكَوَتَعَالَى) — makes mention of you.

---

[18] From the *Hadīth* of Abū Hurayrah — (رَضِيَٱللَّهُعَنْهُ).(2699)

Because the souls are more attached and inclined to this worldly-life, if it is said to a person: "If you do this or that, then governor so and so or president so and so will mention you (in a good way) and he will praise you in front of those in charge;" he will be excited and moved, however, regarding the *Dhikr* of Allāh which will cause us to be mentioned by Allāh, we become weak and lack energy in performing it?! This is due to our negligence, carelessness, weakness, disregard and our lack of giving this matter the concern and importance that it deserves.

IT WILL EARN YOU THE *SALĀH* OF ALLĀH AND THE ANGELS

From the benefits of *Dhikr*—and it is an extension of the previous one—is that the one making *Dhikr* gains, by way of his remembrance of Allāh, the *Salāh* of Allāh and the angels. Allāh — (سُبْحَانَهُوَتَعَالَ) — said:

﴿ يَٰٓأَيُّهَا ٱلَّذِينَ ءَامَنُوا۟ ٱذْكُرُوا۟ ٱللَّهَ ذِكْرًا كَثِيرًا ۝ وَسَبِّحُوهُ بُكْرَةً وَأَصِيلًا ۝ هُوَ ٱلَّذِى يُصَلِّى عَلَيْكُمْ وَمَلَٰٓئِكَتُهُۥ لِيُخْرِجَكُم مِّنَ ٱلظُّلُمَٰتِ إِلَى ٱلنُّورِ ﴾

"O you who believe! Remember Allāh with much remembrance. (41) And glorify His Praises morning and afternoon [the early morning (Fajr) and 'Asr prayers]. (42) He it is Who sends Salāh (His blessings) on you, and His angels too (ask Allāh to bless and forgive you), that He may bring you out from darkness (of disbelief and polytheism) into light (of

Belief and Islāmic Monotheism)." [*Sūrah al-Ahzāb* 33:41-43]

This is a benefit from the benefits of *Dhikr,* and it is that the one making *Dhikr* receives the *Salāh* of Allāh and the angels. And the *Salāh* of Allāh means that Allāh will praise him in the assembly of angels as has proceeded. As for the *Salāh* of the angels, it means that they will make *Du'ā* (supplicate) for him; and the more a person increases in Ēmān (faith), making *Dhikr* of Allāh and becomes stronger in adhering to goodness, the more the angels will supplicate for him. Allāh – (سُبْحَانَهُۥوَتَعَالَىٰ) – said:

﴿ ٱلَّذِينَ يَحۡمِلُونَ ٱلۡعَرۡشَ وَمَنۡ حَوۡلَهُۥ يُسَبِّحُونَ بِحَمۡدِ رَبِّهِمۡ وَيُؤۡمِنُونَ بِهِۦ وَيَسۡتَغۡفِرُونَ لِلَّذِينَ ءَامَنُواْ رَبَّنَا وَسِعۡتَ كُلَّ شَيۡءٍ رَّحۡمَةً وَعِلۡمًا فَٱغۡفِرۡ لِلَّذِينَ تَابُواْ وَٱتَّبَعُواْ سَبِيلَكَ وَقِهِمۡ عَذَابَ ٱلۡجَحِيمِ ۝ رَبَّنَا وَأَدۡخِلۡهُمۡ جَنَّٰتِ عَدۡنٍ ٱلَّتِي وَعَدتَّهُمۡ وَمَن صَلَحَ مِنۡ ءَابَآئِهِمۡ وَأَزۡوَٰجِهِمۡ وَذُرِّيَّٰتِهِمۡ إِنَّكَ

أَنتَ ٱلۡعَزِيزُ ٱلۡحَكِيمُ ۝ وَقِهِمُ ٱلسَّيِّـَٔاتِۚ وَمَن تَقِ ٱلسَّيِّـَٔاتِ يَوۡمَئِذٍ فَقَدۡ رَحِمۡتَهُۥۚ وَذَٰلِكَ هُوَ ٱلۡفَوۡزُ ٱلۡعَظِيمُ ۝

"Those (angels) who bear the Throne (of Allāh) and those around it glorify the praises of their Lord, and believe in Him, and ask forgiveness for those who believe (in the Oneness of Allāh) (saying): "Our Lord! You comprehend all things in mercy and knowledge, so forgive those who repent and follow Your Way, and save them from the torment of the blazing Fire! (7) "Our Lord! And make them enter the 'Adn (Eden) Paradise (everlasting Gardens) which you have promised them, — and to the righteous among their fathers, their wives, and their offspring! Verily, You are the All-Mighty, the All-Wise. (8) "And save them from (the punishment, for what they did of) the sins, and whomsoever You save from (the punishment for what he did of) the sins (i.e. pardon him) that Day, him verily, You have taken into mercy." And that is the supreme success." [Sūrah al-Ghāfir 40:7-9]

This is a long, wonderful and blessed *Du'ā* made by the angles for the believers that make *Dhikr* of Allāh, obey Him and fulfill His commandments – (سُبْحَانَهُوَتَعَالَى).

And here – O successful one – is a question that might come to mind: What is it that made those angels attached to the believers and how did they acquire such a status – continuously and persistently making *Du'ā* for the believers – even though the angles are a different species than that of the humans?

The angels are a different species; they were created from light while humans were created from clay – so their creation is different. But still, Allāh – (تَبَارَكَوَتَعَالَى) – attached the angles to the believers and the reason for this is due to the existence of a strong bond between the believers and the angels: Ēmān in Allāh – (تَبَارَكَوَتَعَالَى). Allāh – (سُبْحَانَهُوَتَعَالَى) – said:

﴿ ٱلَّذِينَ يَحْمِلُونَ ٱلْعَرْشَ وَمَنْ حَوْلَهُ يُسَبِّحُونَ بِحَمْدِ رَبِّهِمْ وَيُؤْمِنُونَ بِهِ ﴾

"Those (angels) who bear the Throne (of Allāh) and those around it glorify the praises

of their Lord, and believe in Him." [*Sūrah al-Ghāfir* 40:7]

This is the bond: glorifying the praises of Allāh and having Ēmān in Him — (عَزَّوَجَلَّ).

So the more a person increases in making *Dhikr* of Allāh, His praise, and his faith in Him, the more the angels will increase in making *Du'ā* for him, seeking forgiveness for him and asking Allāh — (تَبَارَكَوَتَعَالَ) — to grant him *Tawfiq*, steadfastness, entrance into paradise and salvation from the hellfire and other than that from the matters mentioned in the noble Āyah.

DHIKR IS A MEANS TO PROTECT THE TONGUE

Similarly, from the benefits of *Dhikr* is that it is a cause for protecting the tongue.

The scholars mention: "The tongue was only created for speech, so if the *Muslim* does not speak with good — and the best good speech is the *Dhikr* of Allāh — he will speak with evil and wickedness." Thus, whoever's tongue becomes dry from the *Dhikr* of Allāh (i.e., he does not make *Dhikr*) — and refuge is sought with Allāh — he will speak with all types of evil: backbiting, slander, ridicule, mockery, lying, filthiness and what is similar to this. So, if the tongue does not make *Dhikr*, it will be occupied with falsehood; but if it becomes busy with *Dhikr*, the falsehood will leave it. That is why there is nothing that can safeguard and maintain the tongue the way that observance of the *Dhikr* of Allāh can — (تَبَارَكَ وَتَعَالَى).

The *Dhikr* of Allāh — (جَلَّ وَعَلَا) — protects the tongue of a person and safeguards it from falling into backbiting, slander, ridicule, mockery and what is similar to that. This is a tremendous benefit from the benefits of the remembrance of Allāh — (تَبَارَكَ وَتَعَالَى).

DHIKR IS A SIGN OF THE GREATNESS OF THE LOVE THAT ONE HAS FOR ALLĀH

From the benefits of *Dhikr* is that it is a sign of the greatness of the love that the one making *Dhikr* has for Allāh — (تَبَارَكَ وَتَعَالَى).

Some of the people of knowledge said: "The sign of loving Allāh is abundance in making *Dhikr* of Him; for verily, you do not love a thing except that you mention and remember it a lot.

These are some of the marvelous benefits and fruits which the believer gains through remembering Allāh — (تَبَارَكَ وَتَعَالَى). And you when you read — O successful one — the book, *al-Wābil as-Sayyib,* you will find that I extremely fell short and failed to appropriately list the benefits of *Dhikr*; and that what I mentioned is an insignificant amount from the tremendous and numerous benefits which Ibn al-Qayyim — (رَحِمَهُ ٱللَّهُ) — truly excelled in detailing and clarifying.

So, going back to the beginning, I strongly urge with the acquirement of this book and benefiting from it; and that it be circulated in the houses and the children, women, daughters, and relatives be encouraged to read it so that they can gain by way of it the great deal of good, tremendous rewards, shelter and protection and other than that from the few aforementioned benefits.

In conclusion, I will relate a few lines of poetry by the extremely knowledgeable scholar, 'Abdur-Rahmān Ibn Nāsir as-Si'dī—(رَحِمَهُٱللَّهُ). They are small in number and beautiful. He—(رَحِمَهُٱللَّهُ)—masterfully gathered in them the benefits of *Dhikr* with the brevity known for poetry. He said:

فذكرُ إلهِ العرشِ سِرّاً ومعلناً :::: يُزيلُ الشَّقَا والهمَّ عنك ويَطردُ

ويجلُبُ للخيراتِ دنيا وآجلاً :::: وإنْ يأتِكَ الوَسواسُ يوماً يُشَرَّدُ

فقد أخبَرَ المختارُ يوماً لصحبِه :::: بأنَّ كثيرَ الذّكرِ في السَّبق مُفرِدُ

ووَصَّى معاذاً يَستعين إلهه :::: على ذكرِهِ والشكر بالحسن يعبدُ

وأوصى لشخصٍ قد أتى بنصيحةٍ :::: وقد كان في حمْل الشرائع يَجْهَدُ

بأنْ لا يزالَ رطباً لسانُك هذه ::: تُعينُ على كلِّ الأمور وتسعِدُ

وأخبَرَ أنَّ الذِكرَ غَرسٌ لأهلِهِ :::: بجناتِ عَدن والمساكنُ تُمْهَدُ

وأخبَرَ أنَّ الله يذكرُ عبدَهُ :::: ومَعْهُ على كلّ الأمورِ يُسَدّدُ

وأخبَرَ أن الذّكرَ يبقى بجنة ::: وينقطعُ التكليفُ حين يُخلُدوا

ولو لم يكنْ في ذكره غيرَ أنَّه::::: طريقٌ إلى حبّ الإله ومُرشِدُ

وَينهَى الفتى عن غيبةٍ ونميمةٍ ::: وعن كلّ قول للدّيانةِ مُفسِدُ

لكان لنا حظّ عظيمٌ ورغبةٌ ::::: بكثرة ذكر الله نعمَ المُوَحَّدُ

ولكنّنا من جهلنا قلَّ ذكرُنا ::::: كما قلَّ منَّا للإله التَعبُّدُ

Remembrance of the God of the throne inwardly and outwardly – will remove and distance you from misery and worry.

And it will bring you the good of this world and the next – and if the whispers (of Shayṭān) come to you one day, it will chase it away.

The chosen one (Muhammad – (ﷺ)) one day informed his companions – that abundant Dhikr will cause you to join the Mufarridūn (those that constantly remember Allāh)

And he advised Mu'āth (Ibn Jabal – (رضي الله عنه)) to seek assistance from God – in remembering and thanking Him and perfecting His worship.

And he advised a person who came to him for advice – who found the legislation of the religion-heavy:

Keep this tongue of yours moist – it will aid you in all affairs and make you rejoice.

And he said that Dhikr is cultivation for its people – in the gardens of Eden where their abodes will be prepared.

And he mentioned that Allāh will remember his servant – and rectify all of his affairs.

And he mentioned that Dhikr will remain in paradise – but the hardship in performing it will end.

And [it would suffice] if the only [benefit] in Dhikr was that – it is a path to attain God's love and divine direction,

and that it prevents the youth from falling into backbiting, slander – and every speech which ruins [one's] religion,

it would be a tremendous fortune and an encouragement – to perform much Dhikr of Allāh – the excellent One who is singled out in worship.

However, due to our ignorance, our Dhikr has become scarce – just as our worship for God has diminished.

May Allāh have mercy on him and reward him with the best of rewards for these magnificent and beneficial

DHIKR IS A SIGN OF THE GREATNESS OF
THE LOVE THAT ONE HAS FOR ALLĀH

lines of poetry clarifying the benefits of *Dhikr*. Whoever wants to look into its commentary and explanation should read Ibn al-Qayyim's book, *al-Wābil as-Sayyib*, because this book contains detailed explanations of the benefits and lists them and make them clear in the best way along with a clarification of the proofs as well.

We ask Allāh — (عَزَّوَجَلَّ) — to reward the people of knowledge with the best of rewards on our behalf and benefit us with what He has taught us. And we ask Him — (تَبَارَكَوَتَعَالَى) — to assist us in remembering and being grateful to Him and perfecting his worship; and to also grant us refuge from turning away and being heedless; and that He makes us from those that guide others and are themselves guided, and not from the misguided ones who lead others astray.

O Allāh, rectify our religion for us, which is the safeguard of our affairs; and rectify our worldly (affairs), wherein is our livelihood; and rectify our afterlife to which is our return; and make life for us (as a means of) increase in every good and make death (for us) as a rest from every evil.

And Allāh knows best. May Allāh raise the rank of the servant of Allāh – His Messenger, our Prophet, Muhammad – and grant him peace, bless him and confer favors upon and the entirety of his family and companions.

Made in the USA
Middletown, DE
21 April 2021

38068234R00045